MW00508442

RENAL DIET FOR
BEGINNERS

Quick And Easy Recipes For Your Kidney Disease. Stay
Healthy With The Ultimate Renal Diet Cookbook And Enjoy
Amazing Dishes

JOY ELLEDGE

information is without contract or any type of guarantee assurance.

The trademarks that are used are without any consent, and the publication of the trademark is without permission or backing by the trademark owner. All trademarks and brands within this book are for clarifying purposes only and are owned by the owners themselves, not affiliated with this document.

Table of Contents

INTRODUCTION

When renal function is impaired, a renal diet is deficient in sodium, phosphorus, and potassium, three minerals that the body cannot adequately metabolize and flush out (in excess levels).

A renal diet adheres to a few basic principles. The first is that it must be a well-balanced, organic, and long-term diet that is high in whole grains, vitamins, fibers, carbohydrates, omega-3 fats, and fluids. Proteins should be enough, but not too many.

The Renal Diet Cookbook is for people who have been diagnosed with chronic kidney disease (CKD) and want to eat a balanced diet. The book contains basic, step-by-step, and easy-to-follow recipes, as well as for instructions for kidney patients. This guide was created to assist those with CKD in regaining lost weight and enjoying their favorite foods. The terms kidney function and renal function are used to describe how well the kidneys work. A pair of kidneys is born with every healthy person. As a result, when one of the kidneys stopped working, it went unnoticed because the other kidney was still working. However, if the kidney functions continue to deteriorate and hit a level as low as 25%, the situation becomes dangerous for the patients. People with only one working kidney need adequate external therapy and, in the worst-case scenario, a kidney transplant.

Renal Diet Cookbook aided you in learning more about your condition, making good decisions, and staying on track with the basics. We hope you've learned a lot more about your

Renal Diet as a result of this article. We recognize that the quality of our goods and services is just as critical as the quality of our knowledge at the Renal Diet Cookbook.

When several renal cells called nephrons are partially or entirely impaired, they fail to filter blood entering the body properly, resulting in kidney disease. The progressive damage to kidney cells can be caused by several factors, including an acidic or toxic build-up within the kidney over time, genetics, or other kidney-damaging diseases such as hypertension (high blood pressure) or diabetes.

Chronic Kidney Disease (CKD) is a form of kidney disease (CKD)

Chronic kidney disease, or CKD, is a level of kidney failure in which the kidneys are unable to filter the blood properly. The term chronic is used to describe organ damage that occurs over time. As a result, such a stage must be avoided at all costs. As a result, early detection of the disease is critical. The earlier the patient recognizes the seriousness of the case, the more effective steps he will take to address it. If you need to limit potassium, consult your primary care physician or a dietitian. If you need to lower your potassium levels, you can use your food and drink choices to help.

It is a way of eating that protects your kidneys from more harm. It entails limiting a few ingredients and liquids to prevent such minerals from developing in your body. However, as the infection worsens and kidney failure worsens, you must become more vigilant about what you eat and drink.

Many foods fit well in the renal diet, and once you see how many options there are, it won't seem as restrictive or difficult to stick to. The trick is to concentrate on foods that are rich in nutrients, as these make it easier for the kidneys to absorb waste by reducing the amount of waste that the body has to discard. Long-term renal function depends on maintaining and enhancing balance.

BREAKFAST

1. Cheesy Scrambled Eggs with Fresh Herbs

Preparation Time: 15 minutes

Cooking Time: 10 minutes

Servings: 4

Ingredients:

- 3 Eggs
- 2 Egg whites
- ½ cup Cream cheese
- ¼ cup Unsweetened rice milk
- 1 tbsp. green part only Chopped scallion
- 1 tbsp. Chopped fresh tarragon
- 2 tbsps. Unsalted butter
- Ground black pepper to taste

Directions:

1. Whisk the eggs, egg whites, cream cheese, rice milk, scallions, and tarragon. Mix until smooth.
2. Melt the butter in a skillet.
3. Put egg mixture and cook for 5 minutes or until the eggs are thick and curds creamy.
4. Season with pepper and serve.

Nutrition: Calories: 221 Fat: 19g Carb: 3g Protein: 8g Sodium: 193mg Potassium: 140mg Phosphorus: 119mg

2. Turkey and Spinach Scramble on Melba toast

Preparation Time: 5 minutes

Cooking Time: 15 minutes

Servings: 2

Ingredients:

- 1 tsp. Extra virgin olive oil
- 1 cup Raw spinach
- ½ clove, minced Garlic
- 1 tsp. grated Nutmeg
- 1 cup Cooked and diced turkey breast
- 4 slices Melba toast
- 1 tsp. Balsamic vinegar

Directions:

1. Heat a skillet over medium heat and add oil.
2. Add turkey and heat through for 6 to 8 minutes.
3. Add spinach, garlic, and nutmeg and stir-fry for 6 minutes more.
4. Plate up the Melba toast and top with spinach and turkey scramble.
5. Drizzle with balsamic vinegar and serve.

Nutrition: Calories: 301 Fat: 19g Carb: 12g Protein: 19g Sodium: 360mg Potassium: 269mg

Phosphorus: 215mg

3. Berry Chia with Yogurt

Preparation Time: 35 minutes

Cooking Time: 5 minutes

Servings: 4

Ingredients:

- ½ cup chia seeds, dried

- 2 cup Plain yogurt
- 1/3 cup strawberries, chopped
- ¼ cup blackberries
- ¼ cup raspberries
- 4 teaspoons Splenda

Directions:

1. Mix up together Plain yogurt with Splenda, and chia seeds.
2. Transfer the mixture into the serving ramekins (jars) and leave for 35 minutes.
3. After this, add blackberries, raspberries, and strawberries. Mix up the meal well.
4. Serve it immediately or store it in the fridge for up to 2 days.

Nutrition: Calories: 150Fat: 5gCarbs: 19g Protein: 6.8g Sodium: 65mg Potassium: 226mg Phosphorus: 75mg

4. Egg and Veggie Muffins

Preparation Time: 15 minutes

Cooking Time: 20 minutes

Servings: 4

Ingredients:

- 4 Eggs
- 2 Tbsp. Unsweetened rice milk
- ½ chopped Sweet onion
- ½ chopped Red bell pepper
- Pinch red pepper flakes
- Pinch ground black pepper

Directions:

1. Preheat the oven to 350F.
2. Spray 4 muffin pans with cooking spray. Set aside.
3. Whisk the milk, eggs, onion, red pepper, parsley, red pepper flakes, and black pepper until mixed.
4. Pour the egg mixture into prepared muffin pans.
5. Bake until the muffins are puffed and golden, about 18 to 20 minutes. Serve.

Nutrition: Calories: 84 Fat: 5g Carb: 3g Protein: 7g Sodium: 75mg Potassium: 117mg Phosphorus: 110mg

LUNCH

5. Green Palak Paneer

Preparation Time: 5 minutes

Cooking Time: 10 minutes

Servings: 4

Ingredients:

- 1-pound green lettuce
- 2 cups cubed paneer (vegan)
- 2 tablespoons coconut oil
- 1 teaspoon cumin
- 1 chopped up onion
- 1-2 teaspoons hot green chili minced up
- 1 teaspoon minced garlic
- 15 cashews
- 4 tablespoons almond milk
- 1 teaspoon Garam masala
- Flavored vinegar as needed

Directions:

1. Add cashews and almond milk to a blender and blend well.
2. Set your pot to Sauté mode and add coconut oil; allow the oil to heat up.
3. Add cumin seeds, garlic, green chilies, ginger and sauté for 1 minute.
4. Add onion and sauté for 2 minutes.

5. Add chopped green lettuce, flavored vinegar and a cup of water.
6. Lock up the lid and cook on HIGH pressure for 10 minutes.
7. Quick-release the pressure.
8. Add ½ cup of water and blend to a paste.
9. Add cashew paste, paneer and Garam Masala and stir thoroughly.
10. Serve over hot rice!

Nutrition: Calories: 367 Fat: 26g Carbohydrates: 21g Protein: 16g Phosphorus: 110mg Potassium: 117mg Sodium: 75mg

6. Pizza Pitas

Preparation Time: 10 minutes

Cooking Time: 10 minutes

Servings: 1

Ingredients:

- .33 cup of mozzarella cheese
- 2 pieces of pita bread, 6 inches in size
- 6 tsp. of chunky tomato sauce
- 2 cloves of garlic (minced)
- .25 cups of onion, chopped small
- .25 tsp. of red pepper flakes
- .25 cup of bell pepper, chopped small
- 2 ounces of ground pork, lean
- No-stick oil spray
- .5 tsp. of fennel seeds

Directions:

1. Preheat oven to 400.

2. Put the garlic, ground meat, pepper flakes, onion, and bell pepper in a pan. Sauté until cooked.
3. Grease a flat baking pan and put pitas on it. Use the mixture to spread on the pita bread.
4. Spread one tablespoon of the tomato sauce and top with cheese.
5. Bake for five to eight minutes, until the cheese is bubbling.

Nutrition: Calories: 284 Fat: 10g Carbs: 34g Protein: 16g Sodium: 795mg Potassium: 706mg Phosphorus: 416mg

7. Turkey Pinwheels

Preparation Time: 10 minutes

Cooking Time: 15 minutes

Servings: 6

Ingredients:

- 6 toothpicks
- 8 oz. of spring mix salad greens
- 1 ten-inch tortilla
- 2 ounces of thinly sliced deli turkey
- 9 tsp. of whipped cream cheese
- 1 roasted red bell pepper

Directions:

1. Cut the red bell pepper into ten strips about a quarter-inch thick.
2. Spread the whipped cream cheese on the tortilla evenly.
3. Add the salad greens to create a base layer and then lay the turkey on top of it.

4. Space out the red bell pepper strips on top of the turkey.
5. Tuck the end and begin rolling the tortilla inward.
6. Use the toothpicks to hold the roll into place and cut it into six pieces.
7. Serve with the swirl facing upward.

Nutrition: Calories: 206 Fat: 9g Carbs: 21g Protein: 9g Sodium: 533mg Potassium: 145mg Phosphorus: 47mg

DINNER

8. Beef Chili

Preparation Time: 10 minutes

Cooking Time: 30 minutes

Servings: 2

Ingredients:

- 1 diced Onion
- 1 diced Red bell pepper
- 2 cloves, minced Garlic
- 6 oz. Lean ground beef
- 1 tsp. Chili powder
- 1 tsp. Oregano
- 2 tbsps. Extra virgin olive oil
- 1 cup Water
- 1 cup Brown rice
- 1 tbsp. Fresh cilantro to serve

Directions:

1. Soak vegetables in warm water.
2. Boil a pan of water and add rice for 20 minutes.
3. Meanwhile, add the oil to a pan and heat on medium-high heat.
4. Add the pepper, onions, and garlic and sauté for 5 minutes until soft.
5. Remove and set aside.
6. Add the beef to the pan and stir until browned.
7. Put and stir vegetables back into the pan.

8. Now add the chili powder and herbs and the water, cover, and turn the heat down a little to simmer for 15 minutes.
9. Meanwhile, drain the water from the rice and the lid and steam while the chili is cooking.
10. Serve hot with the fresh cilantro sprinkled over the top.

Nutrition: Calories: 459 Fat: 22g Carb: 36g Protein: 22g Sodium: 33mg Potassium: 360mg Phosphorus: 332mg

9. Pork Meatloaf

Preparation Time: 10 minutes

Cooking Time: 50 minutes

Servings: 1

Ingredients:

- 1-pound lean ground beef
- ½ cup Breadcrumbs
- ½ cup Chopped sweet onion
- 1 Egg
- 2 tbsps. Chopped fresh basil
- 1 tsp. Chopped fresh thyme
- 1 tsp. Chopped fresh parsley
- ¼ tsp. Ground black pepper
- 1 tbsp. Brown sugar
- 1 tsp. White vinegar
- ¼ tsp. Garlic powder

Directions:

1. Preheat the oven to 350f.
2. Mix well the breadcrumbs, beef, onion, basil, egg, thyme, parsley, and pepper.

3. Stir the brown sugar, vinegar, and garlic powder in a small bowl.
4. Put the brown sugar mixture evenly over the meat.
5. Bake the meatloaf for about 50 minutes or until it is cooked through.
6. Let the meatloaf stand for 10 minutes and then pour out any accumulated grease.

Nutrition: Calories: 103 Fat: 3g Carb: 7g Protein: 11g Sodium: 87mg Potassium: 190mg Phosphorus: 112mg

10. Apple & Cinnamon Spiced Honey Pork Loin

Preparation time: 20 minutes

Cooking time: 6 hours

Servings: 6

Ingredients

- 1 2-3lb boneless pork loin roast
- ½ teaspoon low-sodium salt
- ¼ teaspoon pepper
- 1 tablespoon canola oil
- 3 medium apples, peeled and sliced
- ¼ cup honey
- 1 small red onion, halved and sliced
- 1 tablespoon ground cinnamon

Directions

1. Season the pork with salt and pepper.
2. Heat the oil in a skillet and brown the pork on all sides.
3. Arrange half the apples in the base of a 4 to 6-quart slow cooker.

4. Top with the honey and remaining apples.
5. Sprinkle with cinnamon and cover.
6. Cover and cook on low for 6-8 hours until the meat is tender.

Nutrition: Calories 290, Fat 10g, Carbs 19g, Protein 29g, Fiber 2g, Potassium 789mg, Sodium 22mg

MAIN DISHES

11. Apple, Ginger, and Rhubarb Muffins

Preparation Time: 15 minutes

Cooking Time: 25 minutes

Servings: 4

Ingredients:

- ½ cup finely ground almonds
- ¼ cup white rice flour
- ½ cup buckwheat flour
- 1/8 cup unrefined raw sugar
- 2 tbsp. arrowroot flour
- 1 tbsp. linseed meal
- 2 tbsp. crystallized ginger, finely chopped
- ½ tsp. ground ginger
- ½ tsp. ground cinnamon
- 2 tsp. gluten-free baking powder
- A pinch of fine sea salt
- 1 small apple, peeled and finely diced
- 1 cup finely chopped rhubarb
- 1/3 cup almond/ rice almond milk
- 1 large egg
- ¼ cup extra virgin olive oil
- 1 tsp. pure vanilla extract

Directions:

1. Set your oven to 350Fgrease an eight-cup muffin tin and line with paper cases.

2. Combine the almond four, linseed meal, ginger and sugar in a mixing bowl. Sieve this mixture over the other flours, spices and baking powder and use a whisk to combine well.
3. Stir in the apple and rhubarb in the flour mixture until evenly coated.
4. In a separate bowl, whisk the almond milk, vanilla, and egg then pour it into the dry mixture. Stir until just combined – don't overwork the batter as this can yield very tough muffins.
5. Scoop the mixture into the arrange muffin tin and top with a few slices of rhubarb. Bake for at least 25 minutes, till they start turning golden or when an inserted toothpick emerges clean.
6. Take off from the oven and let sit for at least 5 minutes before transferring the muffins to a wire rack for further cooling.
7. Serve warm with a glass of squeezed juice.
Enjoy!

Nutrition: Calories: 325 kcal Protein: 6.32 g Fat: 9.82 g Carbohydrates: 55.71 g

12.   Breakfast Sausage and Mushroom Casserole

Preparation Time: 20 minutes

Cooking Time: 45 minutes

Servings: 4

Ingredients:

- 450g of Italian sausage, cooked and crumbled
- Three-fourth cup of coconut almond milk
- 8 ounces of white mushrooms, sliced

- 1 medium onion, finely diced
- 2 Tablespoons of organic ghee
- 6 free-range eggs
- 600g of carrots
- 1 red bell pepper, roasted
- 3/4 tsp. of ground black pepper, divided
- 1 ½ tsp. of sea salt, divided

Directions:

1. Peel and shred the carrots.
2. Take a bowl, fill it with ice-cold water, and soak the carrots in it. Set aside.
3. Peel the roasted bell pepper, remove its seeds and finely dice it.
4. Set the oven 375°F.
5. Get a casserole baking dish and grease it with the organic ghee.
6. Put a skillet over medium flame and cook the mushrooms in it. Cook until the mushrooms are crispy and brown.
7. Take the mushrooms out and mix them with the crumbled sausage.
8. Now sauté the onions in the same skillet. Cook up to the onions are soft and golden. This should take about 4 – 5 minutes.
9. Take the onions out and mix them in the sausage-mushroom mixture.
10. Add the diced bell pepper to the same mixture.
11. Mix well and set aside for a while.
12. Now drain the soaked shredded carrots, put them on a paper towel, and pat dry.

13. Bring the carrots in a bowl and add about a teaspoon of salt and half a teaspoon of ground black pepper to it. Mix well and set aside.
14. Now take a large bowl and crack the eggs in it.
15. Break the eggs and then blend in the coconut almond milk.
16. Stir in the remaining black pepper and salt.
17. Take the greased casserole dish and spread the seasoned carrots evenly in the base of the dish.
18. Next, spread the sausage mixture evenly in the dish.
19. Finally, spread the egg mixture.
20. Now cover the casserole dish using a piece of aluminum foil.
21. Bake for 20 - 30 minutes. To check if the casserole is baked properly, insert a tester in the middle of the casserole, and it should come out clean.
22. Uncover the casserole dish and bake it again, uncovered for 5 - 10 minutes, until the casserole is a little golden on the top.
23. Allow it to cool for 10 minutes.
24. Enjoy!

Nutrition: Calories: 598 kcal Protein: 28.65 g Fat: 36.75 g Carbohydrates: 48.01 g

13.   Yummy Steak Muffins

Preparation Time: 10 minutes

Cooking Time: 20 minutes

Servings: 4

Ingredients:

- 1 cup red bell pepper, diced
- 2 Tablespoons of water

- 8 ounce thin steak, cooked and finely chopped
- ¼ teaspoon of sea salt
- Dash of freshly ground black pepper
- 8 free-range eggs
- 1 cup of finely diced onion

Directions:

1. Set the oven to 350°F
2. Take 8 muffin tins and line then with parchment paper liners.
3. Get a large bowl and crack all the eggs in it.
4. Beat well the eggs.
5. Blend in all the remaining ingredients.
6. Spoon the batter into the arrange muffin tins. Fill three-fourth of each tin.
7. Put the muffin tins in the preheated oven for about 20 minutes, until the muffins are baked and set in the middle.
8. Enjoy!

Nutrition: Calories: 151 kcal Protein: 17.92 g Fat: 7.32 g Carbohydrates: 3.75 g

SNACKS

14.   Spicy Guacamole

Preparation time: 15 minutes

Cooking time: 15 minutes

Servings: 4 (about 3 tablespoons per serving)

Ingredients:

- 1½ tablespoons freshly squeezed lime juice
- 1 tablespoon minced jalapeño pepper, or to taste
- 1 tablespoon minced red onion
- 1 tablespoon chopped fresh cilantro
- 1 garlic clove, minced
- 1/8 to ¼ teaspoon kosher salt
- Freshly ground black pepper

Direction

1. Combine the lime juice, jalapeño, onion, cilantro, garlic, salt, and pepper in a large bowl, and mix well.

Nutrition: Calories: 61; Total Fat: 5g; Saturated Fat: 1g; Cholesterol: 0mg; Sodium: 123mg; Carbohydrates: 4g; Fiber: 2g; Added Sugars: 0g; Protein: 1g; Potassium: 195mg; Vitamin K: 8mcg

15.   Marinated Berries

Preparation time: 5 minutes

Cooking time: 30 minutes

Servings: 4

Ingredients:

- 2 cups fresh strawberries, hulled and quartered
- 1 cup fresh blueberries (optional)
- 2 tablespoons sugar
- 1 tablespoon balsamic vinegar
- 2 tablespoons chopped fresh mint (optional)
- 1/8 teaspoon freshly ground black pepper

Direction

1. Gently toss the strawberries, blueberries (if using), sugar, vinegar, mint (if using), and pepper in a large nonreactive bowl.
2. Let the flavors blend for at least 25 minutes, or as long as 2 hours.

Nutrition: Calories: 73; Total Fat: 8g; Saturated Fat: 8g; Cholesterol: 0mg; Sodium: 4mg; Carbohydrates: 18g; Fiber: 2g; Added Sugars: 6g; Protein: 1g; Potassium: 162mg; Vitamin K: 9mcg

16.   Roasted Broccoli and Cauliflower

Preparation Time: 7 minutes

Cooking Time: 23 minutes

Serving: 6

Ingredients:

- 2 cups broccoli florets
- 2 cups cauliflower florets
- 2 tablespoons olive oil
- 1 tablespoon freshly squeezed lemon juice
- 2 teaspoons Dijon mustard

- ¼ teaspoon garlic powder
- Pinch salt
- 1/8 teaspoon freshly ground black pepper

Direction

1. Preheat the oven to 425°F.
2. On a baking sheet with a lip, combine the broccoli and cauliflower florets in one even layer.
3. In a small bowl, combine the olive oil, lemon juice, mustard, garlic powder, salt, and pepper until well blended and drizzle the mixture over the vegetables. Toss to coat and spread the vegetables out in a single layer again.
4. Roast for 22 minutes. Serve immediately.

Nutrition: 63 Calories 74mg Sodium 39mg Phosphorus 216mg Potassium 2g Protein

17.Pumpkin-Turmeric Latte

Preparation time: 10 minutes

Cooking time: 10 minutes

Servings: 1

Ingredients:

- ½ cup brewed espresso or 1 cup brewed strong coffee
- ¼ cup pumpkin purée
- 1 teaspoon vanilla extract
- 1 teaspoon sugar
- ½ teaspoon ground turmeric
- ½ teaspoon ground cinnamon, plus more if needed
- 1 cup 1% almond milk

Direction

1. Combine the espresso, pumpkin, vanilla, sugar, turmeric, and cinnamon in a medium saucepan over medium heat, whisking occasionally.
2. Warm the almond milk over low heat in a small pan. When it is warm (not hot), whisk it vigorously (or mix with a blender or handheld frother) to make it foamy.
3. Pour the hot coffee mixture into a mug, then top with the frothy almond milk. Sprinkle with more cinnamon, if desired.

Nutrition: Calories: 169; Total Fat: 3g; Saturated Fat: 2g; Cholesterol: 12mg; Sodium: 128mg; Carbohydrates: 26g; Fiber: 3g; Added Sugars: 5g; Protein: 9g; Potassium: 665mg; Vitamin K: 11mcg

SOUP AND STEW

18. Pork Soup

Preparation Time: 10 minutes

Cooking Time: 4 hours 15 minutes

Servings: 8

Ingredients:

- 2 lbs. country pork ribs, boneless and cut into 1-inch pieces
- 2 cups cauliflower rice
- 1 1/2 tbsp. fresh oregano, chopped
- 1 cup of water
- 2 cups Red bell peppers, chopped
- 1 cup chicken stock
- 1/2 cup dry white wine
- 1 onion, chopped
- 3 garlic cloves, chopped
- 1 tbsp. olive oil
- Pepper
- Salt

Directions:

1. Heat oil in a saucepan over medium heat.
2. Season pork with pepper and salt. Add pork into the saucepan and cook until lightly brown from all the sides.
3. Add onion and garlic and saute for 2 minutes.

4. Add Red bell peppers, water, stock, and white wine and stir well. Bring to boil.
5. Pour saucepan mixture into the slow cooker.
6. Cover and cook on high for 4 hours.
7. Add cauliflower rice and oregano in the last 20 minutes of cooking.
8. Stir well and serve.

Nutrition: Calories 263 Fat 15.1 g Carbohydrates 5.8 g Sugar 2.6 g Protein 23.4 g Cholesterol 85 mg Phosphorus: 130mg Potassium: 117mg Sodium: 105mg

19.   Mexican Bean Soup

Preparation time 20mins

Cooking time 25mins,

Serving 4

Ingredients:

- 4 Red bell peppers
- 150 g green beans
- 1 onion
- 1 clove of garlic
- 1 red chili pepper
- 2 tbsp. olive oil
- 2 tbsp. tomato paste
- 1 tsp paprika noble sweet
- 1 tsp ground cumin
- 1 tsp ground coriander
- 1 l vegetable broth
- 240 g kidney beans (can; drained weight)
- 240 g white beans (can; drained weight)
- Salt

- Pepper
- Coriander greens for garnish

Directions:

1. Scald, quench, peel, remove the stalk and roughly chop the Red bell peppers with hot water. Wash the green beans, clean them, and cut them into small pieces.
2. Wash and clean the chili, remove the seeds and, if desired, finely chop it.
3. Sauté onion garlic and chilly. Sauté the tomato paste and add paprika, cumin, and cilantro to the mixture. Put the broth in and bring it to a boil. Add the green beans and Red bell peppers and simmer over low heat for about 10 minutes. The kidney and white beans are drained, washed, and added.
4. Let it simmer more for 5 minutes. Serve in bowls with coriander leaves and season with salt and pepper.

Nutrition: Calories 205 kcal Protein 13 g, Fat 6 g, Carbohydrates 23 g,

20. Chickpea Curry Soup

Preparation Time: 10 minutes

Cooking Time: 25 minutes

Servings: 4

Ingredients:

- ¼ cup extra-virgin olive oil or coconut oil
- 1 medium onion, finely chopped
- 2 garlic cloves, sliced
- 1 large apple, cored, peeled, and cut into ¼-inch dice
- 2 teaspoons curry powder

- 1 teaspoon salt
- 3 cups peeled butternut squash cut into ½-inch dice
- 3 cups vegetable broth
- 1 cup full-fat coconut almond milk
- 1 (15-ounce) can chickpeas, drained and rinsed
- 2 tablespoons finely chopped fresh cilantro

Directions:

1. In a huge pot, heat the oil on high heat.
2. Add the onion and garlic and sauté until the onion begins to brown, 6 to 8 minutes.
3. Put the apple, curry powder, and salt and sauté to toast the curry powder, 1 to 2 minutes.
4. Put the squash and broth then bring to a boil.
5. Lower the heat then cook until the squash is tender about 10 minutes.
6. Stir in the coconut almond milk.
7. Using an immersion blender, purée the soup in the pot until smooth.
8. Stir in the chickpeas and cilantro, heat through for 1 to 2 minutes, and serve.

Nutrition: Calories: 469 Total Fat: 30g Total Carbohydrates: 45g Sugar: 14g Fiber: 10g

Protein: 12g Sodium: 1174mg

VEGETABLE

21.   Chilaquiles

Preparation Time: 20 minutes

Cooking Time: 20 minutes

Servings: 4

Ingredients:

- 3 (8-inch) corn tortillas, cut into strips
- 2 tablespoons of extra-virgin olive oil
- 12 tomatillos, papery covering removed, chopped
- 3 tablespoons for freshly squeezed lime juice
- 1/8 teaspoon of salt
- 1/8 teaspoon of freshly ground black pepper
- 4 large egg whites
- 2 large eggs
- 2 tablespoons of water

44

- 1 cup of shredded pepper jack cheese

Directions:

1. In a dry nonstick skillet, toast the tortilla strips over medium heat until they are crisp, tossing the pan and stirring occasionally. This should take 4 to 6 minutes. Remove the strips from the pan and set aside.
2. In the same skillet, heat the olive oil over medium heat and add the tomatillos, lime juice, salt, and pepper. Cook and frequently stir for about 8 to 10 minutes until the tomatillos break down and form a sauce. Transfer the sauce to a bowl and set aside.
3. In a small bowl, beat the egg whites, eggs, and water and add to the skillet. Cook the eggs for 3 to 4 minutes, stirring occasionally until they are set and cooked to 160°F.
4. Preheat the oven to 400°F.
5. Toss the tortilla strips in the tomatillo sauce and place in a casserole dish. Top with the scrambled eggs and cheese.
6. Bake for 10 to 15 minutes, or until the cheese starts to brown. Serve.

Nutrition: Calories: 312 Total fat: 20g Saturated fat: 8g Sodium: 345mg Phosphorus: 280mg Potassium: 453mg Carbohydrates: 19g Fiber: 3g Protein: 15g Sugar: 5g

22.   Vegetable Confetti

Preparation Time: 25 minutes

Cooking Time: 15 minutes

Servings: 1

Ingredients:

- ½ red bell pepper
- ½ green pepper, boiled and chopped
- 4 scallions, thinly sliced
- ½ tsp. of ground cumin
- 3 tbsp. of vegetable oil
- 1 ½ tbsp. of white wine vinegar
- Black pepper to taste

Directions:

1. Join all fixings and blend well.
2. Chill in the fridge.
3. You can include a large portion of slashed jalapeno pepper for an increasingly fiery blend

Nutrition: Calories: 230   Fat: 25g Fiber: 3g Carbs: 24g Protein: 43g

23.   Vegetable Green Curry

Preparation Time: 20 minutes

Cooking Time: 20 minutes

Servings: 6

Ingredients:

- 2 tablespoons extra-virgin olive oil
- 1 head broccoli, cut into florets
- 1 bunch asparagus, cut into 2-inch lengths
- 3 tablespoons water
- 2 tablespoons green curry paste
- 1 medium eggplant
- 1/8 teaspoon salt
- 1/8 teaspoon freshly ground black pepper
- 2/3 cup plain whole-almond milk yogurt

Directions:

1. Put olive oil in a large saucepan in a medium heat. Add the broccoli and stir-fry for 5 minutes. Add the asparagus and stir-fry for another 3 minutes.
2. Meanwhile, in a small bowl, combine the water with the green curry paste.
3. Add the eggplant, curry-water mixture, salt, and pepper. Stir-fry or until vegetables are all tender.
4. Add the yogurt. Heat through but avoid simmering. Serve.

Nutrition: Calories: 113 Total fat: 6g Saturated fat: 1g Sodium: 174mg Phosphorus: 117mg Potassium: 569mg Carbohydrates: 13g Fiber: 6g Protein: 5g Sugar: 7g

SIDE DISHES

24.   Cinnamon Apple Chips

Preparation Time: 5 minutes

Cooking Time: 2 to 3 hours

Servings: 4

Ingredients:

- 4 apples
- 1 teaspoon ground cinnamon

Directions:

1. Preheat the oven to 200°F. Line a baking sheet with parchment paper.
2. Core the apples and cut into 1/8-inch slices.
3. In a medium bowl, toss the apple slices with the cinnamon. Spread the apples in a single layer on the prepared baking sheet.
4. Cook for 2 to 3 hours, until the apples are dry. They will still be soft while hot, but will crisp once completely cooled.
5. Store in an airtight container for up to four days.
6. Cooking tip: If you don't have parchment paper, use cooking spray to prevent sticking.

Nutrition: Calories: 96; Total Fat: 0g; Saturated Fat: 0g; Cholesterol: 0mg; Carbohydrates: 26g; Fiber: 5g; Protein: 1g; Phosphorus: 0mg; Potassium: 198mg; Sodium: 2mg

25.   Ginger Cauliflower Rice

Preparation Time: 10 minutes

Cooking Time: 10 minutes

Servings: 4

Ingredients:

- 5 cups cauliflower florets
- 3 tablespoons coconut oil
- 4 ginger slices, grated
- 1 tablespoon coconut vinegar
- 3 garlic cloves, minced
- 1 tablespoon chives, minced
- A pinch of sea salt
- Black pepper to taste

Directions:

1. Put cauliflower florets in a food processor and pulse well.
2. Heat up a pan with the oil over medium-high heat, add ginger, stir and cook for 3 minutes.
3. Add cauliflower rice and garlic, stir and cook for 7 minutes.
4. Add salt, black pepper, vinegar, and chives, stir, cook for a few seconds more, divide between plates and serve.
5. Enjoy!

Nutrition: Calories 125, fat 10, 4, fiber 3, 2, carbs 7, 9, protein 2, 7 Phosphorus: 110mg Potassium: 117mg Sodium: 75mg

SALAD

26. Macaroni Salad

Preparationtime:5minutes
Cookingtime:5minutes
Servings: 4

Ingredients:

- ¼ tsp. celery seed
- 2 hard-boiled eggs
- 2 cups salad dressing
- 1 onion
- 2 tsps. white vinegar
- 2 stalks celery
- 2 cups cooked macaroni
- 1 red bell pepper
- 2 tbsps. mustard

Direction:

1. In a bowl add all ingredients and mix well
2. Serve with dressing

Nutrition: Calories 360, Fat 21g, Sodium (Na) 400mg, Carbs 36g, Protein 6g, Potassium (K) 68mg, Phosphorus 36 mg

27. Grapes Jicama Salad

Preparation Time: 5 minutes

Cooking Time: 0 minutes

Servings: 2

Ingredients:

- 1 jicama, peeled and sliced
- 1 carrot, sliced
- 1/2 medium red onion, sliced
- 1 ¼ cup seedless grapes
- 1/3 cup fresh basil leaves
- 1 tablespoon apple cider vinegar
- 1 ½ tablespoon lemon juice
- 1 ½ tablespoon lime juice

Direction:

1. Put all the salad ingredients into a suitable salad bowl.
2. Toss them well and refrigerate for 1 hour.
3. Serve.

Nutrition: Calories 203 Total Fat 0.7g Sodium 44mg Protein 3.7g Calcium 79mg Phosphorous 141mg Potassium 429mg

FISH & SEAFOOD

28.   Marinated Salmon Steak

PreparationTime:10min
CookingTime:10minutes
Servings: 4

Ingredients:

- ¼ cup lime juice
- ¼ cup soy sauce
- 2 tablespoons olive oil
- 1 tablespoon lemon juice
- 2 tablespoons chopped fresh parsley
- 1 clove garlic, minced
- ½ teaspoon chopped fresh oregano
- ½ teaspoon ground black pepper
- 4 (4 ounce) salmon steaks

Directions:

1. In a large non-reactive dish, mix together the lime juice, soy sauce, olive oil, lemon juice, parsley, garlic, oregano, and pepper. Place the salmon steaks in the marinade and turn to coat. Cover, and refrigerate for at least 30 minutes.
2. Preheat grill for high heat.
3. Lightly oil grill grate. Cook the salmon steaks for 5 to 6 minutes, then salmon and baste with the marinade. Cook for an additional 5 minutes, or to desired doneness. Discard any remaining marinade.

Nutrition: Calories 108, Total Fat 8.4g, Saturated Fat 1.2g, Cholesterol 9mg, Sodium 910mg, Total Carbohydrate 3.6g, Dietary Fiber 0.4g, Total Sugars 1.7g, Protein 5.4g, Calcium 19mg, Iron 1mg, Potassium 172mg, Phosphorus 165 mg

29.   Tuna with honey Glaze

PreparationTime:10min
CookingTime:10minutes
Servings: 4

Ingredients:

- 1/4 cup honey
- 2 tablespoons Dijon mustard
- 4 (6 ounce) boneless tuna fillets
- Ground black pepper to taste

Directions:

1. Preheat the oven's broiler and set the oven rack at about 6 inches from the heat source; prepare the rack of a broiler pan with cooking spray.
2. Season the tuna with pepper and arrange onto the prepared broiler pan. Whisk together the honey and Dijon mustard in a small bowl; spoon mixture evenly onto top of salmon fillets.
3. Cook under the preheated broiler until the fish flakes easily with a fork, 10 to 15 minutes.

Nutrition: Calories 160, Total Fat 8.1g, Saturated Fat 0g, Cholesterol 0mg, Sodium 90mg, Total Carbohydrate 17.9g, Dietary Fiber 0.3g, Total Sugars 17.5g, Protein 5.7g, Calcium 6mg, Iron 0mg, Potassium 22mg, Phosphorus 16 mg

30.   Smoked Salmon and Radishes

Preparation Time: 10 minutes

CookingTime:10minutes
Servings: 8

Ingredients:

- ½ c. drained and chopped capers
- 1 lb. skinless, de-boned and flaked smoked salmon
- 4 chopped radishes
- 3 tbsps. Chopped chives
- 3 tbsps. Prepared beet horseradish
- 2 tsps. Grated lemon zest
- 1/3 c. roughly chopped red onion

Directions:

1. In a bowl, combine the salmon while using the beet horseradish, lemon zest, radish, capers, onions and chives, toss and serve cold.
2. Enjoy!

Nutrition: Calories: 254, Fat: 2 g, Carbs: 7 g, Protein: 7 g, Sugars: 1.4 g, Sodium: 660 mg

31.   Parmesan Baked Fish

Preparation Time: 10 minutes

CookingTime:10minutes
Servings: 4

Ingredients:

- ½ tsp. Worcestershire sauce
- 1/3 c. mayonnaise
- 3 tbsps. Freshly grated parmesan cheese
- 4 oz. cod fish fillets
- 1 tbsp. snipped fresh chives

Directions:

1. Preheat oven to 450°C.

2. Rinse fish and pat dry with paper towels; spray an 8x8x2" baking dish with non-stick pan spray, set aside.
3. In small bowl stir mayo, grated cheese, chives, and Worcestershire sauce; spread mixture over fish fillets.
4. Bake, uncovered, 12-15 minutes or until fish flakes easily with a fork

Nutrition: Calories: 850.5, Fat: 24.8g, Carbs: 44.5 g, Protein: 104.6 g, Sugars: 0.6 g, Sodium: 307.7 mg

POULTRY RECIPES

32.   Cilantro Drumsticks

Preparation Time: 12 minutes

Cooking Time: 18 minutes

Servings: 4

Ingredients:

- 8 chicken drumsticks
- ½ cup chimichurri sauce
- ¼ cup lemon juice

Directions:

1. Coat the chicken drumsticks with chimichurri sauce and refrigerate in an airtight container for no less than an hour, ideally overnight.
2. When it's time to cook, pre-heat your fryer to 400°F.
3. Remove the chicken from refrigerator and allow return to room temperature for roughly twenty minutes.
4. Cook for eighteen minutes in the fryer. Drizzle with lemon juice to taste and enjoy.

Nutrition: Calories: 483 Fat: 29g Carbs: 16 g Protein: 36 g Calcium 38mg, Phosphorous 146mg,

Potassium 227mg Sodium: 121 mg

33.   Buckwheat Salad

PreparationTime:12minutes
CookingTime:20minutes
Servings: 3

Ingredients:

- 2 cups water
- 1 clove garlic, smashed
- 1 cup uncooked buckwheat
- 2 large cooked chicken breasts - cut into bite-size pieces
- 1 large red onion, diced
- 1 large green bell pepper, diced
- 1/4 cup chopped fresh parsley
- 1/4 cup chopped fresh chives
- 1/2 teaspoon salt
- 2/3 cup fresh lemon juice
- 1 tablespoon balsamic vinegar
- 1/4 cup olive oil

Directions:

1. Bring the water, garlic to a boil in a saucepan. Stir in the buckwheat, reduce heat to medium-low, cover, and simmer until the buckwheat is tender and the water has been absorbed, 15 to 20 minutes.
2. Discard the garlic clove and scrape the buckwheat into a large bowl.
3. Gently stir the chicken, onion, bell pepper, parsley, chives, and salt into the buckwheat.
4. Sprinkle with the olive oil, balsamic vinegar, and lemon juice. Stir until evenly mixed.

Nutrition: Calories 199, Total Fat 8.3g, Sodium 108mg, Dietary Fiber 2.9g, Total Sugars 2g, Protein 13.6g, Calcium 22mg, Potassium 262mg, Phosphorus 188 mg

34.   Chicken Saute

Preparation Time: 10 minutes

Cooking Time: 25 minutes

Servings: 2

Ingredients:

- 4 oz. chicken fillet
- 4 Red bell peppers, peeled
- 1 bell pepper, chopped
- 1 teaspoon olive oil
- 1 cup of water
- 1 teaspoon salt
- 1 chili pepper, chopped
- ½ teaspoon saffron

Directions:

1. Pour water in the pan and bring it to boil.
2. Meanwhile, chop the chicken fillet.
3. Add the chicken fillet in the boiling water and cook it for 10 minutes or until the chicken is tender.
4. After this, put the chopped bell pepper and chili pepper in the skillet.
5. Add olive oil and roast the vegetables for 3 minutes.
6. Add chopped Red bell peppers and mix up well.
7. Cook the vegetables for 2 minutes more.
8. Then add salt and a ¾ cup of water from chicken.
9. Add chopped chicken fillet and mix up.
10. Cook the saute for 10 minutes over the medium heat.

Nutrition: Calories 192, Fat 7.2 g, Fiber 3.8 g, Carbs 14.4 g, Protein 19.2 g Calcium 79mg, Phosphorous 216mg, Potassium 227mg Sodium: 101 mg

MEAT RECIPES

35. Lamb Keema

Preparation time: 5 min

Cooking Time: 20 minutes

Servings: 4

Ingredients:

- 1 1/2 pounds ground lamb
- 1 onion, finely chopped
- 2 teaspoons garlic powder
- 2 tablespoons garam masala
- 1/8 teaspoon salt
- 3/4 cup chicken broth

Directions:

1. In a large, heavy skillet over medium heat, cook ground lamb until evenly brown.
2. While cooking, break apart with a wooden spoon until crumbled.
3. Transfer cooked lamb to a bowl and drain off all but 1 tablespoon fat. Saute onion until soft and translucent, about 5 minutes.
4. Stir in garlic powder, and sauté 1 minute.
5. Stir in garam masala and cook 1 minute.
6. Return the browned lamb to the pan, and stir in chicken beef broth.
7. Reduce heat, and simmer for 10 to 15 minutes or until meat is fully cooked through, and liquid has evaporated.

Nutrition: Calories 194, Total Fat 7.3g, Saturated Fat 2.6g, Cholesterol 87mg, Sodium 160mg, Total Carbohydrate 2.2g, Dietary Fiber 0.4g, Total Sugars 0.9g, Protein 28.1g, Calcium 18mg, Iron 2mg, Potassium 379mg, Phosphorus 240mg

36.   Lamb Stew with Green Beans

Preparation time: 30 min

Cooking Time: 1 hr.10 minutes

Servings: 4

Ingredients:

- 1 tablespoon olive oil
- 1 large onion, chopped
- 1 stalk green onion, chopped
- 1-pound boneless lamb shoulder, cut into 2-inch pieces
- 3 cups hot water
- ½ pound fresh green beans, trimmed
- 1 tablespoon chopped fresh parsley
- 1/2 teaspoon dried mint
- 1/2 teaspoon dried dill weed
- 1 pinch ground nutmeg
- ¼ teaspoon honey
- Salt and pepper to taste

Directions:

1. Heat oil in a large pot over medium heat. Saute onion and green onion until golden.
2. Stir in lamb, and cook until evenly brown.
3. Stir in water. Reduce heat and simmer for about 1 hour.

4. Stir in green beans. Season with parsley, mint, dill, nutmeg, honey, salt and pepper.
5. Continue cooking until beans are tender.

Nutrition: Calories 81, Total Fat 5.1g, Saturated Fat 1.1g, Cholesterol 19mg, Sodium 20mg, Total Carbohydrate 2.8g, Dietary Fiber 1g, Total Sugars 1g, Protein 6.5g, Calcium 17mg, Iron 1mg, Potassium 136mg, Phosphorus 120mg

37. Chunky Beef and Potato Slow Roast

Preparation Time: 15 minutes

Cooking Time: 5-6 hours

Servings: 12

Ingredients:

- 3 cups of peeled carrots, chunked
- 1 cup of onion
- 2 garlic cloves, chopped
- 1 ¼ pound flat-cut beef brisket, fat trimmed
- 2 cups of water
- 1 teaspoon of chili powder
- 1 tablespoon of dried rosemary

For the sauce:

- 1 tablespoon of freshly grated horseradish
- ½ cup of almond milk (unenriched)
- 1 tablespoon lemon juice (freshly squeezed)
- 1 garlic clove, minced
- A pinch of cayenne pepper

Directions:

1. Double boil the carrots to reduce their potassium content. Chop the onion and the garlic. Place the beef

68

brisket in a slow cooker. Combine water, chopped garlic, chili powder, and rosemary.

2. Pour the mixture over the brisket. Cover and cook on high within 4-5 hours until the meat is very tender. Drain the carrots and add them to the slow cooker.

3. Adjust the heat to high and cook covered until the carrots are tender. Prepare the horseradish sauce by whisking together horseradish, almond milk, lemon juice, minced garlic, and cayenne pepper.

4. Cover and refrigerate. Serve your casserole with a dash of horseradish sauce on the side.

Nutrition: Calories: 199 Protein: 21g Carbohydrates: 12g Fat: 7g Sodium: 282mg Potassium: 317 Phosphorus: 191mg

BROTHS, CONDIMENT AND SEASONING

38. **Berbere Spice Mix**

Preparation Time: 15 minutes

Cooking Time: 4 minutes

Servings: ½ cup

Ingredients:

- 1 tablespoon coriander seeds
- 1 teaspoon cumin seeds
- 1 teaspoon fenugreek seeds
- ¼ teaspoon black peppercorns
- ¼ teaspoon whole allspice berries
- 4 whole cloves
- 4 dried chilis, stemmed and seeded
- ¼ cup dried onion flakes
- 2 tablespoons ground cardamom

- 1 tablespoon sweet paprika
- 1 teaspoon ground ginger
- ½ teaspoon ground nutmeg
- ½ teaspoon ground cinnamon

Directions:

1. Put the coriander, cumin, fenugreek, peppercorns, allspice, and cloves in a small skillet over medium heat. Lightly toast the spices, swirling the skillet frequently, for about 4 minutes or until the spices are fragrant.
2. Remove the skillet, then let the spices cool for about 10 minutes. Transfer the toasted spices to a blender with the chilis and onion, and grind until the mixture is finely ground.
3. Transfer the ground spice mixture to a small bowl and stir together the cardamom, paprika, ginger, nutmeg, and cinnamon until thoroughly combined. Store the spice mixture in a small container with a lid for up to 6 months.

Nutrition: Calories: 8 Fat: 0g Carbohydrates: 2g Phosphorus: 7mg Potassium: 37mg Sodium: 14mg Protein: 0g

39.   Fajita Rub

Preparation Time: 15 minutes

Cooking Time: 0 minutes

Servings: ¼ cup

Ingredients:

- 1½ teaspoons chili powder
- 1 teaspoon garlic powder
- 1 teaspoon roasted cumin seed
- 1 teaspoon dried oregano
- ½ teaspoon ground coriander
- ¼ teaspoon red pepper flakes

Directions:

1. Put the chili powder, garlic powder, cumin seed, oregano, coriander, and red pepper flakes in a blender, pulse until ground and well combined. Transfer the spice mixture and store for up to 6 months.

Nutrition: Calories: 1 Fat: 0g Carbohydrates: 0g Phosphorus: 2mg Potassium: 7mg Sodium: 7mg Protein: 0g

DESSERT

40.   Blueberry swirl cake

Preparation time: 15 minutes

Cooking time: 45 minutes

Servings: 9

Ingredients:

- 1/2 cup margarine
- 1 1/4 cups reduced fat almond milk
- 1 cup granulated sugar
- 1 egg
- 1 egg white
- 1 tbsp. Lemon zest, grated
- 1 tsp. Cinnamon
- 1/3 cup light brown sugar
- 2 1/2 cups fresh blueberries
- 2 1/2 cups self-rising flour

Directions:

1. Cream the margarine and granulated sugar using an electric mixer at high speed until fluffy.
2. Add the egg and egg white and beat for another two minutes.
3. Add the lemon zest and reduce the speed to low.
4. Add the flour with almond milk alternately.
5. In a greased 13x19 pan, spread half of the batter and sprinkle with blueberry on top. Add the remaining batter.
6. Bake in a 350-degree Fahrenheit preheated oven for 45 minutes.
7. Let it cool on a wire rack before slicing and serving.

Nutrition: Calories: 384; carbs: 63g; protein: 7g; fats: 13g; phosphorus: 264mg; potassium: 158mg; sodium: 456mg

41. Blueberry espresso brownies

Preparation time: 15 minutes

Cooking time: 30 minutes

Servings: 12

Ingredients:

- 1/4 cup organic cocoa powder
- 1/4 teaspoon salt
- 1/2 cup raw honey
- 1/2 teaspoon baking soda
- 1 cup blueberries
- 1 cup coconut cream
- 1 tablespoon cinnamon
- 1 tablespoon ground coffee
- 2 teaspoon vanilla extract
- 3 eggs

Directions:

1. Preheat the oven to 3250f.
2. In a bow mix together coconut cream, honey, eggs, cinnamon, honey, vanilla, baking soda, coffee and salt.
3. Use a mixer to combine all ingredients.
4. Fold in the blueberries
5. Pour the batter in a greased baking dish and bake for 30 minutes or until a toothpick inserted in the middle comes out clean.
6. Remove from the oven and let it cool.

Nutrition: Calories: 168; carbs: 20g; protein: 4g; fats: 10g; phosphorus: 79mg; potassium: 169mg; sodium: 129mg

DRINKS AND SMOOTHIES

42.   Cranberry Smoothie

Preparation Time: 10minutes

Cooking Time: 0 minutes

Servings: 1

Ingredients:

- 1 cup frozen cranberries
- 1 medium cucumber, peeled and sliced
- 1 stalk of celery
- Handful of parsley
- Squeeze of lime juice

Directions:

1. First, start by putting all the ingredients in a blender jug. Give it a pulse for 30 seconds until blended well.
2. Serve chilled and fresh.

Nutrition: Calories 126 Protein 12 g Fat 0.03 g Cholesterol 0 mg Potassium 220 mg Calcium 19 mg Fiber 1.4g

43.   Apple and Blueberry Crisp

Preparation Time: 1 hour 10 minutes

Cooking Time: 1 hour

Serving: 8

Ingredients:

- Crisp
- 1/4 cup of brown sugar

- 1 1/4 cups quick cooking rolled oats
- 6 tbsp. non-hydrogenated melted margarine
- 1/4 cup all-purpose flour (unbleached)

Filling:

- 2 tbsp. cornstarch
- 1/2 cup of brown sugar
- 2 cups chopped or grated apples
- cups frozen or fresh blueberries (not thawed)
- 1 tbsp. fresh lemon juice
- 1 tbsp. melted margarine

Directions:

1   Preheat the oven to 350°F with the rack in the middle position.
2   Pour all the dry ingredients into a bowl, then the butter and stir until it is moistened. Set the mixture aside.
3   In an 8-inch (20-cm) square baking dish, mix the cornstarch and brown sugar. Add lemon juice and the rest of the fruits. Toss to blend the mixture. Add the crisp mixture, then bake until the crisp turns golden brown (or for 55 minutes to 1 hour). You can either serve cold or warm.

Nutrition: Calories 127 Fat 2.1g Carbs 18.2g Protein 22.7g Potassium (K) 256mg Sodium (Na) 61mg Phosphorous 28 mg

CONCLUSION

T the number one reason why patients are urged to stay healthy during the early stages of kidney disease is to avoid dialysis for as long as possible.

Each recipe has been carefully crafted by a team of experts who have the knowledge and experience to make sure you get the most out of every meal. All of the recipes in this cookbook have been carefully adjusted to ensure that they contain low levels of sodium, potassium, and phosphorus. This is important because these foods provide the necessary vitamins and minerals for people with kidney failure.

This can be done by incorporating the right types of nutrients in your diet, all of which are included in the right amount, in the renal diet. Maintaining your activity levels, getting enough sleep, and quitting bad habits, such as smoking and alcohol, will support your journey towards staying healthy and avoiding dialysis.

Even though there is no cure for chronic kidney disease, it is a journey that you can manage. You can sustain your health and continue living your life as normal, with a high quality of life, for much longer than if you don't follow these basic guidelines.

The number one thing to remember on this journey is that you are in complete control of your outcome.

A renal diet is tied in with directing the intake of protein and phosphorus in your eating routine. Restricting your sodium intake is likewise significant. By controlling these two variables you can control the vast majority of the toxins/waste made by your body and thus this enables your kidney to 100% function. If you get this early enough and truly moderate your diets with extraordinary consideration, you could avert all-out renal failure. If you get this early, you can take out the issue completely.

Water, herbal tea, lemonade, and fruit juices with no high sugar content are prescribed beverages that will support kidney patients. Sugar has a diuretic effect on the kidneys that can make the disease worse and can lead to dehydration. Kidney patients need fluids, potassium, and sodium, and protein intake to be monitored and recorded. This will help them keep track of changes in their hydration status and deviations in diet that can have negative effects on their health status.

The proper renal diet can help kidneys functioning longer, and it has only more restrictions on proteins and table salt, while restrictions to phosphorous and potassium can be needed if the levels of blood rise and the signs of accumulation become too evident.

Each recipe listed will help you achieve your health and fitness goals and provide most of the nutrients that the body needs to function. Your body won't be deprived of any micronutrient or macronutrient. Low sodium will also assist in striking the right balance between saturated and unsaturated fats.

CPSIA information can be obtained
at www.ICGtesting.com
Printed in the USA
LVHW080931010621
689026LV00009B/1186